War Crimes and the Culture of Peace

Madam Justice Louise Arbour and
Senator Keith Davey

War Crimes and the Culture of Peace

MADAM JUSTICE LOUISE ARBOUR

Published in association with
Victoria University by
University of Toronto Press

© University of Toronto Press Incorporated 2002
Toronto Buffalo London
Printed in Canada

ISBN 0-8020-8495-8

Printed on acid-free paper

The Senator Keith Davey Lecture

National Library of Canada Cataloguing in Publication Data

Arbour, Louise, 1947–
War crimes and the culture of peace

(The Senator Keith Davey lecture)
ISBN 0-8020-8495-8

1. War crime trials.   2. International criminal courts.
I. Title.   II. Series: Senator Keith Davey lecture series.

K5301.A94 2002   341.6'9   C2002-900001-7

University of Toronto Press acknowledges the
financial assistance to its publishing program of the
Canada Council for the Arts and the
Ontario Arts Council.

University of Toronto Press acknowledges the financial
support for its publishing activities of the Government
of Canada through the Book Publishing Industry
Development Program (BPIDP).

Contents

CONCLUDING REMARKS
Closing Remarks

Appreciation

BIOGRAPHICAL NOTES

Preface

THIS IS THE FIFTH ANNUAL LECTURE in honour of Senator Keith Davey.

Disraeli once said that a university should be 'a place of life, of liberty and of learning.' I thank all those present at the lecture and those who read this volume for joining Victoria University and the University of Toronto in realizing that purpose.

This lecture would not be possible were it not for two men: Senator Jerry Grafstein, whose idea it was to establish the lecture and whose efforts made it possible to raise the funds for its endowment, and the Honourable Keith Davey, who is truly a special person.

Not only has he made a significant contribution to Canadian politics, but he has done so in a singular and most admirable fashion. I am certain that everyone will agree. Nobody has ever heard Senator Davey utter an unkind word about anyone. Always positive, always active, he is the ideal man to have on your team. He is one of the keys to the successes of Prime Ministers Pearson and Trudeau! Together with his wise and sensitive wife, Dorothy, they constitute an unbeatable powerhouse. They merit our respect, admiration, and applause.

In introducing Madam Justice Louise Arbour, Chief Justice McMurtry cannot fail to mention that she is a strong, brilliant, compassionate, and dedicated person. This is, however, not quite the whole story, for each of those adjectives requires a superlative, as Madam Justice is one of the strongest, most brilliant, most compassionate, and most dedicated people I know. Since that number includes most of the thousand wonderful people present at the lecture, this is a great compliment indeed.

I have the privilege of thanking the TD Bank Financial Group for its generous support of the lecture and, in particular, of the reception that follows. Mr Michael Foulkes, executive vice-president and a graduate of Victoria University, has been particularly gracious in making this co-operative venture possible.

I would like to thank the University of Toronto Press for publishing the lecture series, the Faculty of Music for allowing us use of the auditorium, the Victoria staff and our student ambassadors who have guided you to the lecture and helped you find seats, the lecture committee which included Senator and Mrs Davey, Alison Broadworth, David Cameron, David Cook, Jon Davies, Larry Davies, Martha Drake, Roger Hutchinson, Brian Merrilees, Robert Vipond, and for Donald Wilson. Most of all I would like to express my gratitude to the Daveys, who have provided inspiration and energy to the committee. They offer us all an active model for participation in civil society, for political leadership, and for wise and dignified statesmanship.

This lecture is one of the most exciting annual events in this country – not only for the outstanding quality of the speakers but for the meteorological uncertainty of January in Canada.

Many people ask me how we select the lecturers. All are brilliant; all have taught at some point; all have had at least two careers and have succeeded not only in Canada but internationally. All have offered us a contribution to the small-l liberal agenda, which includes not only the 'good' society (John Galbraith) but the 'just' society (Louise Arbour).

It has been said that man's capacity for justice makes democracy *possible*, while man's inclination to injustice makes democracy *necessary*. The lecture that follows deals with these issues and with the hope expressed by Abraham Lincoln in his second inaugural address – that we might 'achieve a just and lasting peace among … all nations.'

In a recent book, *The Lion, the Fox and the Eagle*, Carol Off characterized Louise Arbour as the eagle, a *rara avis*. When I hear that word, I always think of Neil Armstrong. When he touched down on the moon he said, 'The Eagle has landed.' Well, Canada's eagle has now returned, and it is wonderful to welcome her back home.

The other speakers today include Dr Heather

Munroe-Blum, vice-president for research and international relations at the University of Toronto and author of an important report on university research in Ontario, and the Honourable Roy McMurtry, chief justice of Ontario, former high commissioner for Canada to Britain. Among so many important positions and functions, he is also a marvellous artist, to whom Victoria University is most grateful for his lovely rendition of historic Burwash Hall in oil on stone, a piece of slate from the original roof! The Honourable Herb Gray, deputy prime minister of Canada, is father of a graduate of Victoria University and was also coordinator of millennium activities for Canada. In that role he joined us in opening the Lester B. Pearson Garden for Peace and Understanding at Victoria University in the autumn of 2000.

The poet Tennyson said, 'At the beginning of the new millennium, ring in the thousand years of peace.' It is therefore appropriate that we begin this century by thinking of the culture of peace.

Roseann Runte

Participants

MADAM JUSTICE LOUISE ARBOUR is a justice of the Supreme Court of Canada. Please see the biographical note on pages 59–60 below.

MICHAEL A. FOULKES is executive vice-president of the TD Bank Financial Group. He is an alumnus of Victoria University.

HON. HERB GRAY, PC, MP, is deputy prime minister of Canada.

CHIEF JUSTICE R. ROY MC MURTRY of Ontario served as attorney general in several Conservative governments in Ontario and as Canada's high commissioner to the United Kingdom.

DR HEATHER MUNROE-BLUM is vice-president for research and international relations in the University of Toronto.

DR ROSEANN RUNTE has been president of Victoria University in the University of Toronto and in mid-2001 became president of Old Dominion University in Norfolk, Virginia.

Opening Remarks

Welcome

DR HEATHER MUNROE-BLUM

SENATOR AND MRS DAVEY, Deputy Prime Minister Gray, Madam Justice Arbour, Chief Justice McMurtry, distinguished guests, friends, and colleagues: on behalf of President Bob Birgeneau, myself, and the University of Toronto it gives me extraordinary pleasure to welcome you to the annual Keith Davey Lecture at Victoria University in the University of Toronto.

Today's lecture represents one in a series of superb lectures given in honour of our great senator. I recall distinctly the first Davey lecture, when John Kenneth Galbraith stood before a packed room and delivered a brilliant address. The crowded auditorium contrasted with the blustering snowstorm outside, which was stalling traffic and bringing the rest of Toronto to a halt. By comparison, the weather today is beautiful, but the guest lecturer equally distinguished, and the room, as always, packed. You have an enormous treat in store for you. The University of Toronto is deeply honoured to have Madam Justice Arbour in our midst.

Let me also take this opportunity to say a few words about Victoria University's president, Roseann Runte. Given her departure to Old Dominion University, in Norfolk, Virginia, this may be my last opportunity to recognize her in the context of the Davey lecture. Roseann Runte has brought inspired leadership to her role as president. She is a wise, deeply intelligent, thoughtful, and elegant leader. She has contributed enormously over her tenure as president. She has been gracious and confident in her leadership. She will be greatly missed.

Let me close by extending again the welcome of the University of Toronto to this distinguished event.

Introduction

CHIEF JUSTICE
R. ROY MC MURTRY

I AM DELIGHTED TO BE once again a guest for the annual Senator Keith Davey Lecture and particularly to have been invited to introduce the distinguished guest lecturer. The lecture has become a very significant cultural occasion in our city, and Victoria University is to be congratulated for hosting this important event.

As one who was once a member of a political party different from that of Senator Davey, I am therefore confident that I cannot be accused of political partisanship when I express once again the appreciation of his fellow citizens for his most unique and valuable contribution to the public life of Canada over many years. I am very pleased therefore to be here to honour Keith Davey and his wife, Dorothy, and to wish them many more years of continued happiness.

It is indeed a pleasure now to introduce my good friend and former colleague on the Ontario Court of Appeal, the Honourable Madam Justice Louise Arbour. As a result of her distinguished international service and her appointment to the Supreme Court of Canada, Justice Arbour has become one of our country's most celebrated citizens. Indeed, her entire professional career has been simply outstanding.

Louise Arbour was born and educated in Quebec and on her graduation from the University of Montreal's Faculty of Law became a law clerk for Mr Justice Louis-Phillippe Pizem of the Supreme Court of Canada. At that time, she regarded herself as a unilingual francophone, but she quickly achieved extraordinary fluency in Canada's second official language. Most English-speaking lawyers and judges, including me, would be ecstatic if they could be as articulate in their first language as she is in her second.

After serving as a member of the Criminal

Procedure Project at the federal Law Reform Commission, Louise Arbour became a law professor at Osgoode Hall Law School, where she taught for thirteen years before leaving her post as associate dean to accept an appointment to the Supreme Court of Ontario in 1987. Three years later, Justice Arbour was named to the Ontario Court of Appeal.

In 1995, the federal government appointed Justice Arbour to conduct an inquiry into certain highly publicized and disturbing events at the Prison for Women in Kingston, Ontario. In 1996, as we all know, the Security Council of the United Nations named her chief prosecutor for the International Criminal Tribunals for the former Yugoslavia and for Rwanda.

Her courageous service has been well documented and universally applauded. Furthermore, her role was a major influence in the development of an international consensus for a permanent International War Crimes Tribunal. It is significant that U.S. President Bill Clinton, in one of his last official duties, has made an executive decision that the United States is to participate in the process of the tribunal that is to be constituted.

In September 1999, Madam Justice Arbour

became a member of the Supreme Court of Canada.

As we listen to Justice Arbour's lecture, 'War Crimes and the Culture of Peace,' we all should recognize that there are very few people who have observed as closely as our lecturer the horrors and barbarism fuelled by extreme ethnic and cultural nationalism. There are lessons to be learned continually by every nation on earth about the perils of extreme nationalism, including, of course, Canada.

Justice Arbour has already helped to educate the international community as to why strangers in peril in distant lands should be everyone's business. For most of human history the boundaries of our moral universe have been the borders of tribe, language, religion, or nation. The idea that we have obligations to people beyond our borders simply because they are fellow human beings is a relatively recent innovation. The result is our awakening to the shame of having done less than we could have to help the millions of strangers who suffered and perished in the twentieth century's experiments in terror and extermination.

Indeed, people around the world have been inspired by Justice Arbour's commitment to a more universal human rights culture and to the necessity for the moral connections that this new culture helps us to create.

It therefore gives me great pleasure to invite you to read the incisive words of the Honourable Madam Justice Louise Arbour.

The Senator Keith Davey Lecture

War Crimes and the Culture of Peace

MADAM JUSTICE LOUISE ARBOUR

O N 4 SEPTEMBER 1998, Jean Kambanda, former prime minister of Rwanda, pleaded guilty before an international tribunal to genocide, conspiracy, public incitement, and complicity in genocide and in the crimes against humanity of murder and extermination, thereby admitting his role in the extermination of over half a million of his own people. After reviewing the terms of the plea agreement between Kambanda and the Office of the Pros-

Delivered in the MacMillan Auditorium, University of Toronto, 11 January 2001; original text available at http://vicu.utoronto.ca

ecutor, which included detailed admissions of the particulars of his participation in the genocide, the Trial Chamber of the International Criminal Tribunal for Rwanda (ICTR) accepted his guilty plea and sentenced him to life imprisonment.

In reviewing the factors that could serve to mitigate the severity of the sentence, the Trial Chamber made the following observation: '50. According to the Prosecutor, Jean Kambanda had expressed his intention to plead guilty immediately upon his arrest and transfer to the Tribunal, on 18 July 1997. Jean Kambanda declared in the Plea Agreement that he had resolved to plead guilty even before his arrest in Kenya and that his prime motivation for pleading guilty was the profound desire to tell the truth, as the truth was the only way to restoring national unity and reconciliation in Rwanda. Jean Kambanda condemned the massacres that occurred in Rwanda and considers his confession as a contribution towards the restoration of peace in Rwanda' (ICTR-97-23-S).

In October 2000, the ICTR's Appeals Chamber dismissed his appeal challenging the validity of his guilty plea and the length of his sentence (ICTR-97-23-A).

I have long thought that Kambanda's guilty plea was the single most important event in the emerging history of the two international courts with which I have been associated – the International Criminal Tribunal for the former Yugoslavia (ICTY) and its sister institution for Rwanda (ICTR). Yet it received very little attention, at least in the European and North American press. Even in Africa, the public impact did not in my view reflect the magnitude of this extraordinary legal precedent. In part, this low profile results, I now believe, from the nature of the process itself, and it has triggered for me a much broader reflection about the role of international criminal law and the need to develop a procedural framework that is adapted to its unique mission and mode of operation.

The method of resolving criminal charges by way of a plea of guilty by the defendant is a common, indeed preferred method of disposition of criminal charges in common law–based, adversarial systems. When an accused is prepared to concede his or her culpability vis-à-vis the charges brought by the prosecution, the court need ensure merely that the plea is voluntary and informed and that the defendant understands that he or she waives a right to insist that the prosecution meet its onerous burden of proof. The court must also be satisfied that the facts alleged by the prosecution and conceded by the defendant satisfy the legal requirements of the charge. There is usually no independent public interest in deploying the whole dramatic performance of a trial to tell the story. Even less so is there any requirement, even within an adversarial-style trial, that the prosecution paint the full and rich context that would permit a deep understanding of the causes of a particular crime, of its type of crime, and of crime more generally.

When Jean Kambanda pleaded guilty at the ICTR, his public admission of guilt was certainly a major blow to the revisionism that was already implanting itself not so much in Rwanda as in neighbouring countries. But it inevitably prevented emergence of a forum in which the complex story of the Rwandan genocide could begin to be told, believed and understood.

Linking Criminal Accountability and Peace

Prosecutions for war crimes and genocide are not ordinary prosecutions. On 25 May 1993, the Security Council of the United Nations, having concluded that the continued massive violations of international humanitarian law in the former Yugoslavia constituted a threat to international peace and security, acted under chapter 7 of the UN Charter to establish an international criminal tribunal mandated to investigate and prosecute persons responsible for such violations and, in doing so, to contribute to the restoration and maintenance of peace. Having found that the situation in Rwanda continued to constitute a threat to international peace and security, the Security Council on 8 November 1994, by a similar resolution, created another ad hoc tribunal, charging it not only with helping to restore and maintain peace but also with aiding the process of national reconciliation in Rwanda.

The link between criminal accountability and peace was essential to the juridical foundation of the intervention by the Security Council. In order to avail itself of chapter 7 of the UN Charter, thereby overriding state sovereignty and mandating states, often against their will, to take or to refrain from taking certain actions, the Security Council was bound by law to find a threat to world peace and to enact a measure – in this case, for the first time ever, a measure of personal criminal accountability – that would serve to re-establish the disturbed world peace. How, one may ask, can criminal justice contribute to the promotion of peace? More particularly, as I ask in the second part of this lecture, how can we structure international criminal trials for war crimes, crimes against humanity, and genocide so that they promote a culture of peace? But first, a brief overview of where these two institutions now stand.

The International Criminal Tribunal for the Former Yugoslavia (ICTY)

The ICTY, located in The Hague, currently employs twelve hundred staff members from seventy-five countries. Fourteen judges, each from a different country, preside over the proceedings. A yearly budget of approximately U.S. $95 million was available to it in 1999 and 2000, in contrast to the original U.S. $10 million in 1994. The ICTY is mandated to prosecute and try persons responsible for grave breaches of the Geneva Conventions of 1949 and of their additional protocols of 1977; for violations of the laws or customs of war; for genocide; and for crimes against humanity. The tribunal's jurisdiction concerns such crimes committed in former Yugoslavia since 1991. Its jurisdiction is open-ended in time and can be terminated only by a resolution of the Security Council.

Ninety-six individuals have been publicly indicted since the ICTY's creation. Two have pleaded guilty, one was acquitted, and eighteen indictments were withdrawn. Eight indictees died, most of natural causes, but one accused committed suicide while at the UN detention unit in the Netherlands, and three were killed while resisting arrest. There have been so far twelve convictions, among which three were maintained on appeal, and the others are currently before the ICTY's Appeals Chamber.

Of the accused whose public indictment is still outstanding as I speak, twenty-seven are still at large, including Slobodan Milosevič and his four co-accused, as well as Radovan Karadič and Radko Mladič, whose indictments and arrest warrants have been outstanding for over five years. Arrest warrants were issued to the states where the suspects were believed to be located, and many international arrest warrants were issued as well. Those who are before the tribunal were either arrested by national police authorities or detained by the Stabilization Forces (SFOR – the international forces in Bosnia) and formally arrested there by officials of the tribunal. Some surrendered voluntarily to the ICTY in Croatia and in Bosnia, including, yesterday, 10 January 2001, Biljana Plavsič, former president of the Republika Srpska (RS). Thirty-five accused are currently detained at the UN Detention Unit in the Netherlands, and four have been provisionally released while awaiting trial. The length of the trials held has varied from 79 to 223 days. Most of the charges concerned violations of laws or customs of war, crimes against humanity, and grave breaches of the Geneva Conventions. There have been nineteen accused indicted for sexual offences and nine charges of genocide.

Both the accused and the prosecution regularly avail themselves of the appeal process. There have been three final decisions rendered on appeal. Dusko Tadič received a sentence of twenty years of imprisonment, having been found guilty on several counts of violations of laws or customs of war, crimes against humanity, and grave breaches of the Geneva Conventions. The ICTY sentenced Zlatko Aleksovski to seven years' imprisonment for a violation of the laws or customs of war. Anto Furundzija received ten years following a finding of guilt on two counts of violations of the laws or customs of war, which included torture and rape.

In March 2000, the ICTY found General Tihomic Blaskič, at the time colonel in the HVO – the Bosnian Croat army – guilty on twenty counts of crimes against humanity and war crimes and sentenced him to forty-five years. He is appealing that judgment and sentence.

In May 1999, the ICTY on behalf of the international community indicted a serving head of state – Slobodan Milosevič, president of the Federal Republic of Yugoslavia (FRY) – for crimes against humanity and for violations of the laws or customs of war. It charged him, along with three other members of the Socialist Party of Serbia, including the president of Serbia, and the chief of the general staff of the Armed Forces of the FRY (the Yugoslav army, or VJ), with three counts of crimes against humanity and one count of war crimes. The charges invoke the individual responsibility of each accused, as well as their criminal responsibility for the acts of their subordinates. The indictment results from the large-scale plan to secure, by criminal means, continued Serbian control over the province of Kosovo. The police and armed forces of the FRY and Serbia forcibly expelled and internally displaced from their homes Kosovo Albanians. These forces stole or destroyed the property of the Kosovo Albanians in a systematic manner – they shelled their villages, burned their houses, seized and destroyed their personal identity documents, went from house to house to order the residents to leave, and murdered many of them, including women and children, in the process. They carried out a full-fledged campaign of terror and violence directed at Kosovo Albanians. The ICTY charged the five accused for their participation in planning, preparing, and executing massive deportations, murders, and persecution on political, racial, and religious grounds.

The International Criminal Tribunal for Rwanda (ICTR)

The ICTR, located in Arusha, Tanzania, currently employs seven hundred staff members from eighty countries. As in the case of the tribunal for Yugoslavia, fourteen judges, each from a different country, preside over its proceedings. A total budget of approximately U.S. $80 million was available to it for the year 2000.

The ICTR's mandate is to prosecute and try persons responsible for genocide and other serious violations of international humanitarian law committed in the territory of Rwanda from January to December 1994. It may also try Rwandan citizens charged with such crimes committed on the territory of neighbouring states during the same period. As in the case of the ICTY, persons convicted by this international court will serve their sentences in countries that have entered into agreements with the tribunal to administer such sentences. The ICTR prefers that the sentences that it imposes be served in Africa. Benin, Mali, and Swaziland have signed facilitating agreements. The United Nations Detention Facility (UNDF) was established in 1996 in Arusha as a totally self-standing unit, under the exclusive care and control of the UN.

The UNDF currently holds forty-four detainees. They include several former senior cabinet ministers in Rwanda's interim government of 1994, former military commanders, political leaders, journalists, and senior businessmen. Thirty-six are awaiting either trial or a trial decision; five have been convicted, and their appeal is now pending; and three cases have been fully completed. In May 2000, Belgian national Georges Ruggiu, the only non-Rwandan charged before the ICTR, pleaded guilty to one count of having directly and publicly incited genocide through his radio broadcasts and one count of persecution, a crime against humanity. In June he was sentenced to twelve years of imprisonment, and he did not appeal. Businessman Omar Serushago pleaded guilty to one count of genocide and three counts of crimes against humanity – namely, murder, extermination, and torture. He was sentenced to fifteen years of imprisonment; the ICTR's Appeals Chamber dismissed his appeal on sentence in February 2000.

Shortly after the guilty plea of Jean Kambanda in October 1998, the ICTR found Jean-Paul Akayesu, who was in charge of a commune, as *bourgemeister*, guilty on several counts of genocide, extermination, murder, torture, rape, and other inhumane acts. It acquitted him on other counts involving violations of common article 3 of the Geneva Conventions. His sentence was life imprisonment.

Both the accused and the prosecution appealed. The convictions of Kambanda and Akayesu were the first ever by an international court for the crime of genocide.

Towards an International Criminal Law

I believe that the jurisprudence of the ICTY and of the ICTR provides a sound foundation, based on concrete experience, for the elaboration of the principles of international criminal law. The focus of the work until now has been to build a functioning institution and to create an operational judicial forum that can process cases to their ultimate disposition: the guilt or innocence of the accused. Now we need to establish an international criminal law that will punish, deter, and expose such high crimes against humanity and thereby promote rethinking, reconciliation, and peace.

The ad hoc character of the ICTY and the ICTR has allowed them to concentrate on the job at hand, which in itself was no small task. But the prospect of a soon-to-be-permanent international criminal court, with a much broadened jurisdiction – a prospect that President Clinton invigorated a few days ago by signing the Rome Treaty on the last day that the document was open for signature – will no doubt provoke a deeper search for the theoretical foundations of international criminal justice. My experience with the ad hoc tribunals has persuaded me of the need to develop international criminal law as an autonomous discipline, with its own set of rules and principles that reflect its unique mission and the peculiar environment in which it operates. It will inevitably be a hybrid discipline, torn between the assumptions, often contradictory, of its principal sources and pressed to reflect or at least to accommodate the cultural tenets of the world's dominant legal systems.

I have elaborated on several occasions the difficulties inherent in attempting to merge the two disciplines – public international law and criminal law – that permit the enforcement of international humanitarian law through criminal sanctions. Public international law has its origins in the regulation of interstate relations and is traditionally consensual. It prefers the principle to the rule; it reflects concepts and traditions that come from a variety of legal systems; and it is respectful of the interests of states and sensitive to political factors. Criminal law, by contrast, is coercive, authoritarian, and rigorous. It deals with details – particular facts and specific rules. It is generally not accustomed to the methods of comparative law. The practice of criminal law treats political factors as at best irrelevant and, at worst, offensive and dangerous.

Yet ultimately there are fundamental considerations common to both branches of the law. Both strive to uphold individual rights; both are grounded in the affirmation of basic, shared moral values as well as in the need to preserve order and peace in society. Merging them is a challenge complicated by the inevitable clash of different legal traditions. In civil and commercial matters, economic and commercial imperatives have bridged many of the distinctions between national legal systems. The criminal process has received less cross-fertilization. Criminal trials held in common law jurisdictions remain very different from those in civil law jurisdictions.

Organizing Principle

In light of this situation, the organizing principle for choosing procedural models for the permanent court, as well as for the ad hoc tribunals, should, in my view be the link between personal criminal accountability and peace. This is not a great stretch for criminal law. Although we do not usually think of domestic criminal law as a measure designed to restore or maintain peace, the Anglo–American tradition conceives crime as a breach of the peace. This is why a police officer is called a peace officer. My own familiarity with this terminology and, more important, with its rationale explained my puzzlement when I was told in Bosnia that I should not call on NATO troops to assist in the arrest of indicted war criminals. As it was often put to me, 'Peacekeepers are not police officers.' I thought that they were.

National rules reflect not only a specific reality but also historical and cultural imperatives that are largely immutable but not necessarily exportable – the jury system being a prime example. Exporting the rules without exporting their rationale is of limited assistance.

The international scene is more than the sum of its different parts. It is more, for instance, than all states joined together in the struggle against international organized crime. Transnational efforts – bilateral or multilateral initiatives – can combat the international drug trade and money laundering. But for the investigation and prosecution of crimes against humanity and genocide, we must elaborate an indigenous and original international penal law, both substantively and in matters of process. I believe that we must do so boldly, searching less for the existing common ground than for original measures that will develop new expectations, spreading the culture of peace.

Gary J. Bass, in his excellent recent book *Stay the Hand of Vengeance: The Politics of War Crimes Tribunals* (Princeton, NJ: Princeton University Press, 2000), argues (20–6) that liberal states – the only states that truly champion the idea of war crimes trials – view these trials as a natural extension of the idea of universal rights, which is itself the cornerstone of rights-based democratic regimes. I agree entirely with Bass that modern international war crimes trials, both in reality and in principle, will have to reflect Western prerequisites of due process, such as, first and foremost, the possibility of an acquittal, as well as standards of proof, the right to a defence and to legal assistance, and proportionality of punishment.

This is what I would call the existing common ground. No one argues for less-than-fair war crimes trials, as we understand the notion of fairness, because those who would are in effect arguing for no trials at all.

A Unique Process

What I would like to address briefly is less the common ground – the modicum of fairness and due process that reflects the Western legal necessity at the root of this international judicial adventure – but rather the uniqueness of the international project and, more pointedly, the uniqueness of the war crimes trial itself. Even if we did so only to measure the performance of these institutions, we must articulate realistic expectations about what criminal justice can and should attempt to accomplish internationally. And we must do so within a framework that does not simply mimic our assumptions about the role of criminal law within our own societies.

In the early stages of the launching of the tribunals, the main rationale often advanced for their existence was that they were to be an instrument not only of peace, but of reconciliation among people, by removing the taint that the crimes of their leaders imposed on entire populations. It is argued that the imposition of personal criminal responsibility on leaders will serve to remove the legacy of collective guilt and responsibility. That argument, in my view, is only partly persuasive. First, it is not all that convincing when the persons targeted for prosecution were elected leaders who enjoyed sustained support from the population while their widespread and systematic crimes were unfolding in a blatant and widely reported manner. Of course there are circumstances where repressed or manipulated populations become simply unwilling, and therefore unable, to see even the most obvious truths. Second, this rationale becomes even more problematic when the criminal activities engineered or tolerated by the leaders required the massive participation of large segments of the population – for example, during the genocide in Rwanda. Finally, it is unconvincing when the leaders' crimes advanced group claims of entitlement, based, for instance, on alleged unsettled historical grievances or, worse, on assertions of racial, ethnic, or religious superiority.

I would suggest that, in addition to this

rationale for leaders' personal criminal responsibility, the holding of an international trial is
in itself a major positive step towards peace
and reconciliation. Not that the trial process
itself has an immediate calming effect – quite
the opposite. The issuance of indictments, the
arrest of indictees, and the unfolding of the
story in the dramatic stage of an international
courtroom disturb the semblance of peace that
comes sometimes from ignorance, often from
silence. But more even than the punishment of
the perpetrator, it is the process itself, from
beginning to end, that speaks the language of
peace. The integrity of the criminal justice system in Canada, and in many other countries, is
so well entrenched that we easily forget what it
tells us about who we are and how we live.

Our willingness to submit our disputes to
legal process and, more important, to forgo all
responses to injury except those sanctioned by
law, is the hallmark of our choice to live in
peace with each other. It is exceedingly rare in
domestic criminal law that, regardless of its
outcome, a criminal trial does not suffice to
'stay the hand of vengeance.' Gary Bass chose
that expression as his title, referring to the way
U.S. Justice Robert Jackson so powerfully

expressed this idea in his opening statement at Nuremberg: 'That four great nations, flushed with victory and stung with injury, stay the hand of vengeance and voluntarily submit their captive enemies to the judgment of the law is one of the most significant tributes that Power has ever paid to Reason.'

Finding a Model

If we are to realize this vision, it seems to me that we must make a fundamental choice about the type of trial that should be the norm before an international criminal jurisdiction. There are two broad options. One is to assert modest objectives for the trial itself. It is already a monumental task to reconstitute the crime in its narrow technical conception: the planning, for example, and the execution of the massive homicides, in the predefined legal circumstances that make those killings a crime within international competence. This is already a daunting task in the hyper-sceptical and hyper-critical environment in which this kind of criminal court must operate. The overall strategy would therefore be to proceed in a narrowly focused, clinical fashion, apparently oblivious to any issue that is not directly relevant to the guilt or innocence of the particular individual charged. So the dictates of that model would be to keep it always as simple as possible and to move expeditiously to the final disposition of every individual case.

The second model is to commit the process to the exposition of the larger picture, to painting the broad and complex historical fresco, in an effort not only to expose and record individual guilt but to exploit the dramatic stage of the trial to construct the collective memories that may help cleanse both victims and perpetrators, indeed whole nations, of their brutal past. (For a compelling advocacy of this model, see Mark Osiel, *Mass Atrocity, Collective Memory, and the Law* [New Brunswick, NJ: Transaction Publishers, 1997].)

Considering the nature of the crimes under scrutiny and the efforts invested in prosecuting them internationally, the second model has considerable appeal. A commitment to that model, however, has serious implications that we must articulate and accept at the outset as the inevitable cost of such an ambitious project. For the criminal trial to undertake this historical task, some of the traditional assumptions and requirements of domestic criminal justice as we understand it may require substantial modification.

Furthermore, we must determine whether it is realistic for a criminal prosecutor to undertake the task of a historian. Criminal prosecution is considerably more threatening than history for populations that have already constructed collective memories in which courtroom-quality truth does not constitute a major ingredient. History leaves room for doubt. It is a fluid project, a story in motion, which strives for a reconstruction of the past informed, understood, and therefore revised in the light of the present and even of the future. Justice, in contrast, imposes irreversible conclusions. It binds itself to a permanent and official interpretation of facts, often followed by irreversibly harsh consequences. It favours detailed reconstructions of well-defined, narrowly based events, to a high standard of proof, in order to satisfy its own need for finality. It must keep to a minimum the need for revision and, worse, the possibility of error, both for the sake of those who would have suffered the irreversible consequences of the judgment and for the sake of the credibility, and therefore of the ongoing legitimacy, of the justice project itself. At the same time, the real possibility of the criminal trial's producing an acquittal – a *sine qua non* of fair process – seems an affront to historical accuracy, since the acquittal will be portrayed by some as an official repudiation of all that was alleged by the prosecution, including the context that the law made relevant to culpability. Let me turn to concrete examples of these tensions.

The ICTY has the power to prosecute persons responsible for grave breaches of the Geneva Conventions. In order to prove such grave breaches – which would include, for example, murder and rape – the prosecution must demonstrate that the forbidden acts occurred in the context of an international armed conflict. Therefore this requirement is made part of the offence, and consequently of the charge, by the way in which the tribunal's jurisdiction is defined. Because the criminal burden of proof applies to all elements of an offence, it must be proved beyond a reasonable doubt that the crimes were committed during an international armed conflict. International law has a lot to say about when an armed conflict can be said to be international in nature. This may require, for instance, proof of the involvement of a foreign army to a defined degree. This kind of factual assertion is not the standard fare of criminal trials as we know them and would typically be documented by historians and military analysts, rather than by criminal lawyers. In the case of *Prosecutor* v. *Tadič*, IT-94-1, the ICTY's Trial Chamber found that the conflict in former Yugoslavia was not of an international character at the times relevant to the charges. Accordingly, it acquitted Tadič on several counts, although the Appeals Chamber eventually reversed this finding.

In a similar fashion, the ICTR has jurisdiction to prosecute violations of common article 3 of the Geneva Conventions – namely, war crimes occurring in the context of armed conflicts not of an international character, or, in other words, *internal* armed conflicts. In the case of *Prosecutor* v. *Akayesu*, ICTR-96-4-T, the Trial Chamber found that it was proved beyond a reasonable doubt that such a conflict was taking place in Rwanda. However, the court held that in order to secure a conviction, the prosecution also had to prove beyond a reasonable doubt that Akayesu was either a member of the armed forces under the military command of either of the belligerent parties or that he was legitimately mandated and expected, as a public official or person otherwise holding public authority or de facto representing the government, to support or fulfil the war efforts. The court decided that this requirement was not fulfilled and that it was not shown that the acts perpetrated by the accused were committed in conjunction with the armed conflict. As a result, it acquitted Jean-Paul Akayesu of the counts related to violations of the Geneva Conventions. The prosecution has appealed this ruling, while Akayesu appealed his convictions on other counts.

In both these cases, the legal characterization of the conflict does not relate significantly to the accused's moral culpability. If we were concerned exclusively with personal criminal liability, it is arguable that in the event of a mischaracterization of the nature of the conflict by the tribunal, no miscarriage of justice would occur, as long as the prosecution proved beyond a reasonable doubt that the accused had committed the individual acts of which he was charged, with the requisite prohibited intent. And yet what legitimacy – in fact, what point – would there be for the international community to prosecute a Mr Tadič or a Mr Akayesu if their alleged crimes could not be linked to the disturbance of international peace that involved the international intervention in the first place? Shouldn't the tribunals expose the truth and, in doing so, characterize the historical context appropriately? But can they?

Mark Osiel observed (*Mass Atrocity*, 95–6) that jurisdictional or legal requirements of criminal charges can in fact create major historical distortions. He gives as an example the requirement in the London Charter, which created the Nuremberg Tribunal, allowing prosecution of crimes against humanity only if they were undertaken in preparation for, and in service of, aggressive war. 'This jurisdictional peculiarity required prosecutors to weave the Holocaust into a larger story that was primarily about perverted militarism' (96). In order to overcome these distortions and remain true to the full purpose of international criminal trials, Osiel argues, prosecutors must take a broad view of relevance and expose as much of the context as will serve to displace a focus required solely by legal imperatives.

A Broader Purpose

On 9 December 1946, Brigadier-General Telford Taylor, chief of counsel for the prosecution before Military Tribunal 1 in Nuremberg, made his opening statement in case no. 1, officially designated *United States of America* v. *Carl Brandt et al*. That case, against the twenty-three defendants, was to become known as 'the medical case' or 'the doctors' trial.' Taylor said:

It is owed, not only to the victims and to the parents and children of the victims, that just punishment be imposed on the guilty, but also to the defendants that they be accorded a fair hearing and decision. Such responsibilities are the ordinary burden of any tribunal. Far wider are the duties which we must fulfill here ...

The defendants in the dock are charged with murder but this is no mere murder trial. We cannot rest content when we have shown that crimes were committed and that certain persons committed them ...

It is our deep obligation to all peoples of the world to show why and how these things happened. It is incumbent upon us to set forth with conspicuous clarity the ideas and motives which moved these defendants to treat their fellow men as less than beasts. The perverse thoughts and distorted concepts which brought about these savageries are not dead. They cannot be killed by force of arms. They must not become a spreading cancer in the breast of humanity. (Cited in George J. Annas and Michael A. Grodin, *The Nazi Doctors and the Nuremberg Code: Human Rights in Human Experimentation* [Oxford: Oxford University Press, 1992], 67–8)

Fifteen of the twenty-three defendants were found guilty, and seven, including four physicians, were sentenced to death by hanging. In reviewing the evidence, the tribunal concluded that the experiments that formed the basis of the charges of war crimes and crimes against humanity 'were performed in complete disregard of international interventions, the laws and customs of war, the general principles of criminal law as derived from the criminal laws of all civilized nations' (Annas and Grodin, *The Nazi Doctors*, 104). The tribunal recognized the legitimacy and the legality of certain forms of medical experimentation on human beings and expressed the existence of a consensus that certain basic principles must be observed 'in order to satisfy moral, ethical and legal concepts' (102). The tribunal then proceeded to enunciate the ten basic principles of human experimentation that became known as the Nuremberg Code.

Commenting on the significance of the articulation of a code of medical research in the context of a criminal trial, Michael Grodin observed:

The 10 principles articulating the acceptable limits of human experimentation must be understood in the context of the criminal trials. Nazi physicians and scientists had carried out extensive human experimentation during the war ... The appropriate standards for the conduct of human experimentation were a major theme recurring throughout the trial. While the Tribunal's focus was on the criminal nature of the Nazi experiments, the judges were also grappling with much broader concerns regarding medical research. The trial court sought a historical framework of medical standards from which to judge the Nazi physicians and attempted to elucidate the scope of medical experimentation undertaken by the Nazis, and other physicians and scientists, during World War II ...

The Nuremberg Code was not the first code of human experimentation, nor was it the most comprehensive ... Perhaps it was the unprecedented nature of the atrocities committed by Nazi physicians that has made the Nuremberg Code the hallmark for all subsequent discourse on the ethics of human experimentation. Because the code was written in response to the acts of a scientific and medical community out of control, it is not surprising that voluntary informed consent was its critical centerpiece and the protection of human subjects its paramount concern. (*The Nazi Doctors*, 121–2)

This is probably the most compelling case for a conception of investigations, prosecutions, and trials before international courts, which embrace a purpose much larger than most domestic criminal trials. That conception must translate into sets of rules of procedure and evidence that have sufficient breadth to foster that objective without compromising the guarantees of fairness to individual defendants, without which there can be no recourse to personal criminal responsibility. This broad purpose should be our standard for evaluating the work of international judicial institutions. It should prevent the villification of individual defendants to the point of writing off the entire enterprise if they are not tried and convicted, and it should also resist the pressure for the speediest disposition of the largest number of cases.

Having said that, I must acknowledge that

the doctors' trial opened on 9 December 1946, less than a month after the defendants were charged by indictment. All the evidence in the case had been tendered by 3 July 1947, and, after hearing the personal statements of the defendants and the closing argument of counsel, the court began its deliberations on 19 July and delivered its judgments, including the Nuremberg Code, on 20 August. This was truly a different era in criminal litigation.

Punish, Deter, Understand

In addition to the virtues of speedy disposition, there are many lessons emerging from the modern international efforts of criminal prosecution. They will continue to demonstrate that personal criminal responsibility for war crimes and for crimes against humanity can find its proper place as an integrated measure, at play with other forms of international intervention, by which to promote peace and ensure for all holders of human rights an appropriate balance between security and liberty. Liberal democracies have long been engaged in the search for that proper balance, described by Herbert Packer in *The Limits of the Criminal Sanction*

(Stanford: Stanford University Press, 1968), 65: 'Law, including the criminal law, must in a free society be judged ultimately on the basis of its success in promoting human autonomy and the capacity for individual human growth and development. The prevention of crime is an essential aspect of the environmental protection required if autonomy is to flourish. It is, however, a negative aspect and one which, pursued with single-minded zeal, may end up creating an environment in which all are safe but none is free.'

In searching for an appropriate foundation for the emerging discipline of international criminal justice, we have little to fear from the overreach of legal repressive measures. Packer's concerns were directed at powerful states, not at failed ones. International criminal law reaches out to those who live in states where none are safe and none are free.

Yet when we activate the most repressive form of legal intervention, and, more important, when we have to use repressive legal measures such as criminal penalties, it is critical to remember that the ultimate goal of law in a free society is to liberate rather than to restrain (66). Packer adds: 'The singular power of the criminal law resides ... not in its coercive effect on those caught in its toils but rather in its effect on the rest of us. That effect, I have tried to show, is a highly complex one. It includes elements of coercion and of terror: if I do as he did, I too shall suffer for it. But it also includes conscious and unconscious moralizing and habit-forming effects that go far beyond the crassness of a narrowly conceived deterrence' (69).

This conception of the aim of the criminal sanction does not reduce it to an exact measurement of its potential deterrent effect, even if such measurement were feasible. Rather, it serves to affirm a shared preference for law-abiding conduct, which then becomes the basis on which a community of like-minded individuals, or nations, is formed and nurtured. In addition to relying on classic deterrence by threats, it relies on the appetite, and indeed the basic need, for belonging. In that context, it is truly astonishing that powerful perpetrators of atrocities have not only remained unpunished over the years, but that they have not even been ostracized. It is the 'them among us' that must be addressed through the exposition of their crimes, because as long as they are among us, we are them.

If we exploit the full potential of criminal trials for war crimes, we should do so in part to punish, in part to deter, but, most importantly, to try to understand.

Concluding Remarks

Closing Remarks

DEPUTY PRIME MINISTER
HERB GRAY

IT IS A PARTICULAR HONOUR for me this afternoon to bring your thanks to our distinguished guest speaker. First, a word of explanation as to why I am here today. It is not so much the millennium mentioned by Dr Runte as the fact that I am the father of a fairly recent Victoria graduate. And of course we have to begin by thanking another (somewhat less recent) Victoria graduate, Senator Keith Davey, and his friends for making possible this wonderful annual event.

This lecture series shows that there must not be any barriers between the world of academe and the public square. We need each to inspire and support the other, and this is no more manifest than in the inspired words of our guest lecturer. Another of our leaders, former Prime Minister John Turner, said that human rights have no borders. But those rights, unless they are defined, unless they are enforced, cannot have any meaning.

Our guest speaker has shown the importance of the concept of human rights' having no borders by leaving the bench to enter a world where rights are destroyed, a world in need of sanctions against those who deny those rights. As a great Canadian, she has shown the best of our country, bringing to bear our two great legal traditions, the civil code and the common law, and demonstrating how we work together in an atmosphere of peace. In her work she has exemplified the words of the prophet Zechariah, who said – and I paraphrase freely – that in order to have justice one must have truth and one must have peace. In her work as war crimes prosecutor, in her work as a member first of the Court of Appeal and now of our Supreme Court, she shows how peace requires justice and how justice requires truth. For this, on your behalf, I thank her most sincerely.

Appreciation

MICHAEL A. FOULKES

First of all, I would like to thank Dr Runte for organizing this lecture and the Honourable Senator and Mrs Davey for making the lecture series possible so that we could all enjoy the presence of one of the real, live, modern-day heroes of Canada – our very special guest, Madam Justice Arbour.

Being an alumnus of Victoria University is quite daunting when I consider that the list of graduates reads like a Who's Who? of Canada's literary and financial elite. And it is very fitting that today's lecture took place at the alma mater of Lester B. Pearson, who won the Nobel Peace Prize for suggesting the use of a

United Nations force as a peacekeeper in the Middle East, and of Margaret Atwood, who recently won the Booker Prize for her novel *The Blind Assassin*. In Madam Justice, we have a combination of both their talents – Mr Pearson's passion for peace and Ms Atwood's extraordinary ability to express her views.

It is rare that we have the opportunity to honour a person who has made a mark on the world stage and who at the same time has made us feel proud of those very intangible things that we think of as being uniquely Canadian. When you addressed the Millennium Convocation of the University of Victoria last April, Madam Justice, you put it best: 'There is no better time for Canadians to become global citizens. Because of our differences we are exporters of ideas and ideals'. Well, Madam Justice, most of us are Walter Mittys when it comes to that noble dream. We fantasize about it, and we romanticize it, but *you actually did it*. We were transfixed by the nightly news and the newspaper reports that showed you daring, in your own words, to 'put tyranny on trial.' We felt proud of this wonderfully feisty Canadian who could stare down the perpetrators of some of the most unspeakable crimes against humanity – and not flinch. We admired what has been called your 'impatience and tenaciousness.' We saw courage, determination, and brilliance in your strategy. You made the world sit up and pay attention. You made an enormous difference. You helped us understand that crimes are committed by individuals, not by states or abstract entities. Carol Off, in her book on generals and justice in Rwanda and Yugoslavia – *The Lion, the Fox and the Eagle* – labelled you 'the eagle.' Indeed you were – and we cheered from the sidelines.

So widespread is your influence that the internet's Google search engine has over 9,000 references to you. In browsing through that impressive body of material, we see through your writings and speeches your insights into the evolution of the international human rights process. You have shown us that we are now in an era when justice must be a partner to peace and security. You have made us realize that we need to use the institutions of democracy and justice to create a safe environment, an environment that tolerates dissent and difference. And in doing so we can eradicate the fear that you believe motivates both the oppressed and their oppressors.

We are fortunate to live in Canada's tolerant and peaceful society. But even here you have begun to show us, through your work at the Supreme Court, that there are other ways of looking at things that we take for granted. You are still showing us that there is room for change and a place for a dissenting voice. We have a lot to learn from you.

So it is my honour to thank Madam Justice, one of the rarest of the rare in Canada, a living icon.

Biographical Notes

Madam Justice Louise Arbour

B ORN IN MONTREAL, Louise Arbour received her BA from the Collège Régina Assumpta and her LLL from the Faculté de droit of the Université de Montréal. She taught at Osgoode Hall Law School, York University, from 1974 to 1987 and was associate dean there in 1987. She was appointed that year to the Supreme Court of Ontario (High Court Justice) and in 1990 to the Court of Appeal for Ontario. She was commissioner to conduct an inquiry into certain events at the Prison for Women in Kingston, Ontario, in 1995.

Madam Justice Arbour came to international attention in October 1996 when the Security

Council of the United Nations named her chief prosecutor for the International Criminal Tribunals for the former Yugoslavia and for Rwanda. On 15 September 1999 she was appointed to the Supreme Court of Canada.

Throughout her career, Madam Justice Arbour has published extensively in criminal procedure, criminal law, human rights, civil liberties, and gender issues. She holds honorary degrees from Laurentian University, the Law Society of Upper Canada, the Université du Québec à Montréal, the University of New Brunswick, the University of Ottawa, and York University.

Senator Keith Davey

B ORN IN TORONTO on 21 April 1926, the same day as Princess (now Queen) Elizabeth in Britain, Keith Davey was the son of Charles 'Scotty' Minto Davey and Grace Viola Curtis. He attended North Toronto Collegiate Institute, graduating in 1946 and going on to Victoria University, where he received a BA in 1949. He was an excellent student and president of the student council, although in his typically self-deprecating fashion he recalls that at one point his grades were so poor that he had to surrender the Senior Stick. His humility prevented him from noting that the prized honour was awarded to the student

Senator Keith Davey

with the highest grades who also participated actively in campus life.

Following his graduation from university and a brief stint at the Faculty of Law, Keith Davey went to work for Foster Hewitt and CKFH radio station in sales, rapidly becoming sales manager, a position that he would hold for eleven years.

In 1960 Keith Davey ventured into Canadian politics as campaign organizer for his home riding of Eglinton in Toronto. Having already served as president of Toronto and York's Young Liberal Association, he became national organizer of the Liberal Party in 1961. From 1962 to 1984 he was chair or co-chair of eight national Liberal election campaigns. *Globe and Mail* columnist Scott Young dubbed him 'The Rainmaker' in honour of his ability to precipitate votes for his favourite candidates. Senator Davey would later use this title for his political memoir, *The Rainmaker: A Passion for Politics,* which was published in 1986.

In 1966, Keith Davey was appointed to the Senate by Prime Minister Lester B. Pearson. His various contributions there included chairing the important Senate Committee on Mass Media. He worked closely with Prime Ministers Pearson and Trudeau, offering political advice and sharing warm and loyal friendships.

On his retirement from the upper house in 1996, his colleagues, under the leadership of Senator Jerry Grafstein, raised funds to honour his contribution to Canada and to its political life by establishing a lecture series in his honour at Victoria University. Although Keith Davey retired from the Senate before the required age, he has not left public life and is still active in politics and in his commitment as a family man and avid sports fan. He is married to Dorothy Elizabeth Speare, and they have three children, Catherine, Douglas, and Ian; eight grandchildren; and countless friends.

The Senator Keith Davey Lectures

John Kenneth Galbraith
The Socially Concerned Today
(University of Toronto Press, 1997)

Michael Ignatieff
'The Liberal Imagination: A Defence'
January 1998

Ruud Lubbers
*Revitalizing Liberal Values
in a Globalizing World*
(University of Toronto Press, 1999)

Lord Roy Jenkins
The British Liberal Tradition
(University of Toronto Press, 2001)

Madam Justice Louise Arbour
War Crimes and the Culture of Peace
(University of Toronto Press, 2002)

Hon. Lloyd Axworthy
'Liberals at the Border:
We Stand on Guard for Whom?'
March 2002